# DAKAR

## The Challenge of the Desert

### Experience the world's greatest motorsport event

RallyRaid UK

CYHOEDDWYR
DINEFWR
PUBLISHERS

Published by
Dinefwr Publishers
Rawlings Road, Llandybie, Carmarthenshire
Wales, UK. SA18 3YD
Telephone Sales: (01269) 851989
E-mail: dinefwr.press@btopenworld.com

A CIP catalogue record for this book is
available from the British Library.


ISBN  1 904323 04 9


Printed and bound in Wales by
Dinefwr Press Ltd.
Rawlings Road, Llandybie
Carmarthenshire, SA18 3YD

This book is dedicated to
John Deacon

'You should have seen him'

# contents

Introduction                                8

Foreword                                   10

History                                    14

The Twenty-fifth Dakar Rally              20

Taking part                                36

Vehicles                                   42

Costs                                      46

Finding the money                         48

Support                                    50

Documents and visas                       54

Safety equipment                          55

Signing on and scrutineering              56

Navigation                                 60
    full colour road book
    daily road book
    G.P.S.
    distance trip meter

Daily route                                70

Bivouac                                    79
    food
    information

Fatigue management                         86

Medical                                    89

Vehicle maintenance                        90
    tyres
    Euromaster
    fuel
    Total-Fina-Elf

World press                               100

Communications                            102
    photographs
    press
    clippings

Decision                                  104

Success                                   108

Getting home                              116

Sponsors                                  118

Appendices                                119
    results
    acknowledgements
    useful addresses

## Introduction
By Bill Deacon, father of John William Deacon.

John was interested in sport from his earliest school years and excelled at many of them. When my wife Eva and I bought John his first motorcycle on his sixteenth birthday, we could see that John had found a pastime that would totally absorb him.

From the very beginning, John had already ridden my off-road bikes and had no interest in riding on the road. Very quickly he became involved in local and national enduro events, always riding a four stroke, and progressed very rapidly to become British Four Stroke

John Deacon

Champion. As well as being British Champion he was proud to represent his country for eleven years at the International Six Days Enduro where he won nine gold medals.

It was while he was competing in the World Enduro Championships that John became interested in desert rallies. Although it was clear that he could excel in either of these branches of off-road motorcycle sport he decided to focus on desert rallying However, he still found time to take part in enduro events whenever his busy schedule allowed. John's time was certainly very valuable, being married, running a successful motorcycle dealership and fulfiling competition commitments.

John, ever cheerful, coped with all these demands on his time and never lost sight of his aim to provide an example for newcomers to his chosen sport. It is with pride that I watched him give advice and the benefit of his experience to anybody who asked.

His dedication and hard work led to success that was recognised by BMW when in September 1999 he was signed as a works rider for desert rallies. By this time John had progressed well in these events and in particular in the 'Dakar Rally', which had always been his long-term ambition to win. He was the first British competitor to have a stage win in that event, an achievement that has not yet been repeated.

John was dedicated to encouraging more British competitors to become involved in desert rallying and set up his own school 'Adventure tours' to develop this. He also ran a similar operation on behalf of BMW. His obvious riding skills and his easygoing manner and willingness to help others impressed those who met John in the role of teacher and advisor. They talked about how approachable John was and how willing he was to give advice on any subject.

With these thoughts in mind I am sure that John would have found this book particularly interesting. It has the aim of introducing and clarifying the details of his sport so that others can become more informed and involved. This was one of the tasks that he had set for himself.

John died in Syria while competing in the Master Rally, his 'warm-up' event for the Dakar 2002, where he was aiming for an overall win. His wife Tracey, children James and Zoë, myself, his mother Eva, brother Rob, sister Elizabeth and all his extended family, too numerous to name here, remember John with love and pride.

His motto was: "Don't think about a dream – get out there and DO it". We strongly recommend this thought to the readers of this book.

*Bill Deacon*

Bill Deacon, April 2003

9

# Foreword

## Beauty of life

The Dakar and other rally raids do not leave anybody cold. For some behind their comfortable desks and at a safe distance from the tough action scene, rallying represents an ultimate arrogant show off in front of the poorest people on the planet. After fifteen years of desert events I see things differently.

The desert has humbled me. I don't have illusions anymore about any power that I wield in life. One can't measure life with a stopwatch. I realise now that the rules of successful teamwork need to be applied to the entire human family on the face of the earth. Those children who are watching us go by in front of their mud huts are our sisters and brothers. The fact that they have no shoes and their tee shirts are full of holes does not reduce in the slightest their unique human value. Fascination is glimmering in their eyes when they watch our colourful circus go by. Thoughts get airborne. Without hope and dreams man has no future. Those children along the rally route have already been deprived of most material things. At worst their life is a monotonous struggle for their daily ration of food, wood and water. Why deprive them of the entertainment of the year?

Ari Vatanen and co-driver Tina Thorner during the 2003 event

Africa has taught me the beauty of life. In my mind are engraved the breathtaking shapes of virgin dunes that couldn't possibly have been drawn by human hand. Those lines and the only tree in the middle of them can only come from His Hand. What about those rugged mountains which emerge from soft sand? Their rough and abrasive skin is in stark contrast with the background and it makes me think of the Beauty and the Beast.
The Sahara seems to be endless and man feels so small. He can never conquer the sea, the mountains or the desert. He can never dictate his rule over them. The power of nature will prevail. Yet he will try.

Mankind must do unreasonable things. We must jump into an unknown. We must believe in our convictions however irrational they may seem to be; otherwise life will not advance. Columbus did not ask his neighbours what they thought of his chances of finding a new land on the other side of ocean. Life will reward those who dare to live to the full, with fully blown sails. Only then do you realise that life is incredibly beautiful – because it is so fragile. But we only see beyond the horizon with our hearts.

Ari Vatanen, May 2003

# Ari Vatanen

Ari Vatanen is one of the most famous rally drivers who began his rally career with Ford in 1976. He was born in a famous town in Finland, the name of which was used for the Carelia Suite by Sebelius, a favourite of music lovers. He drove a Peugeot in his first attempt at the Dakar and won the event and could have won again the following year had his car not been stolen during the night. The following two years saw two more wins for Peugeot before switching to Citroën and winning once again.

His record of four car wins in five drives has not yet been equalled. In 1997 he won the World Cross-Country Rally Cup and has won twenty-one events. This success is mirrored in Stage Rallying with nine WRC wins and with World and British Championships.

He was happy to be returning to the Dakar in 2003 as part of the Nissan team from South Africa and quickly proved that he has lost none of his skill. His two stage wins brought the total to forty-nine, a record that will be very hard to beat. Previously regarded as one of the most diplomatic drivers he now uses those skills as a Member of the European Parliament.

Ari Vatanen driving his Peugeot to victory in 1987

# Hubert Auriol

Hubert Auriol is passionate about the Dakar and is now the Director-General of the event. He was one of the most successful competitors and is the only person to have won on two and four wheels. Competing at first on a motorcycle he won on his third attempt using a BMW flat twin. After nine years on two wheels riding Yamaha, BMW and Cagiva machinery he switched to cars. It took another five years before he succeeded in a Mitsubishi and won the rally. Then followed a two-year association with Citroën and their famous buggies in which he achieved a second and third place. His sixteen years experience as a competitor is a valuable asset to the organisation. He greets every competitor on the starting ramp and is at the finish to congratulate all the finishers as they ride onto the podium.

Auriol starts the 25th edition

Auriol drives his BMW to victory in 1983

Auriol forces his Mitsubishi to victory in 1992

## History

Back in 1979 Thierry Sabine could not have realised what he was starting when he inaugurated the first 'Paris to Dakar Rally'. Thierry, an intrepid explorer, had roamed the deserts of North Africa for many years, often accompanied by fellow lovers of 'wild places'. It was the enthusiasm of these friends that led him to consider running an organised event with classes for different types of vehicles.

Recognising the need for financial and organisational help he approached the French newspaper publisher, L'Equipe. Their advice was that the best timing for this type of activity would be during the winter when there were few major international sporting

The Marreau brothers drove a colourful Renault 4 in 1980

events. This led to the adoption of January as the preferred date, a good decision when the temperatures in the North African deserts are taken into consideration.

The 'Thierry Sabine Organisation' (TSO) was born and would continue to organise the event even after Thierry's unfortunate death in a helicopter crash. Later a name change came about when TSO was absorbed into ASO (Amaury Sport Organisation) owned by L'Equipe who are the organisers of other major sporting events. These include the 'Tour de France' cycle race, the 'Le Tourquet' motorcycle beach race and the Paris Marathon and Paris Half Marathon.

As the organisation was changing so was the nature of the event itself. Paris had always been the starting point 'of choice' as the Dakar is very much a French event. Even in the city the actual location of the start area has changed several times. The organisers were always flexible and listened to the requests from various towns south of the capital. These towns were eager to be the location of an overnight stop or failing this even just have the event pass through. For the first ten years the route remained almost the same, however the 'Paris Dakar Rally' was gaining prestige and a lot of places were eager to share in the success. After leaving Paris the competitors would drive south to Marseille where they boarded a ship for North Africa, disembarking in Algeria and then travelling through various North West African countries to the finish at Dakar in Senegal. During this period a pattern emerged whereby the entries reached a high of six hundred competitors with only twenty percent reaching the finish.

From 1989 onwards the courses varied each year, crossing to Tunisia, Libya or Morocco instead of Algeria. This change was brought about by civil unrest in Algeria and once this change had been accepted the organisers grasped the opportunity to vary the route each year. The first big change came in 1992 when the Paris-Le Cap Rallye went all the way to South Africa. This was followed in 1994 by the Paris-Dakar-Paris, a there and back course, the longest ever at thirteen thousand kilometres. This compared with the shortest courses of nine thousand kilometres.

The next change came in 1995 when the starting point was moved to Granada, in southern Spain. This proved a popular decision with the competitors as the long drive down through France, which even though the route was mainly tarmac, in bad

Shinozuka carefully steers his Mitsubishi through a river in the 1997 event

conditions could be a problem. Another innovative change came in 1997 when the event started and finished in Africa at Dakar.

All these changes meant that including 'Paris' in the title was no longer meaningful so the name changed to simply 'Dakar'. The organisers felt that the single word without the attached 'rally' was sufficient. During the twenty-five years that it has been run the 'Dakar' has visited almost every country down the western side of Africa. The most visited country, except for Senegal which is usually the finishing point, is Niger which has hosted part of the 'Dakar' route on twenty occasions. The central Sahara region of Chad, Niger and Mali holds no terrors for the organisers who always treat it with the respect it deserves. Their task is to continually find varied and challenging routes in a harsh environment that is frequently disturbed by civil unrest. For the twenty-fifth Dakar a new route was proposed with the start at Marseille and the finish at the Red Sea resort of Sharm El Sheikh in Egypt.

Following the low percentages of finishers during the first ten years, the next fifteen has shown a rise to fifty percent. There could be many reasons for this: vehicles with improved reliability, superior navigation equipment, teams who are better prepared. There could be many others but the most likely is that the quality of the competitors has improved. From a high of more than six hundred in 1998 the numbers have settled at half that level. The higher numbers of the eighties were probably made up of people that were just 'having a go', possibly using unsuitable vehicles and lacking the necessary skills.

A quarter of a century after Thierry Sabine organised the first event, the 'Dakar' has not only survived, it is thriving. The higher profile brought about by the attention of the world media and the big spending vehicle manufacturers have produced a stronger organisation. This has evolved and grown organically from within. Many of the main organisation roles have been filled by successful competitors from the past. Men like Hubert Auriol and Patrick Zaniroli are now returning some of their experience to the sport.

The most important aspect of this world famous event is the human experiences that all competitors and officials will remember. There is something about the experience that keeps competitors returning year on year to endure, commit and with sheer will power arrive at the finish. It is one of the few remaining international motorsport events where an amateur has the opportunity to compete alongside world champions. What is certain is that the 'Dakar' will continue to flourish; that the course will change constantly and for the amateur and professional alike it will always be an achievement to simply finish. Those competitors that are lucky enough to finish in the top ten positions in any of the classes deserve our admiration.

# Stephane Peterhansel

Frenchman Stephane Peterhansel is one of the most successful off-road motorcyclists of all time. Early in his career he changed from riding for the Husqvarna team to take up a contract with Yamaha France and has been associated with this team since that time. He is the winner of many enduro championships and in 2001 added yet another World championship to his impressive collection when he lifted the 250 four stroke title.

His first attempt in the Dakar in 1988 resulted in a finish in eighteenth place and just three years later he celebrated his first of six wins on his twin cylinder Yamaha. He then decided to try the event on four wheels and after a brief period with a French team using Mega buggies he drove a Nissan pickup in 2001. Now as a member of the strong Mitsubishi team he looks set to be the second competitor to win the Dakar on bikes and in cars. He nearly managed to achieve this double when this year (2003) he was leading until the very last stage only to damage the car and finish in third place. It is only a matter of time.

Peterhansel on the way to his first win in 1991

# The Twenty-Fifth Dakar
1st-19th January 2003

The twenty-fifth milestone event was always going to be different. The organisers who traditionally don't release details of the intended route until late summer announced a new and exciting course. During the last few years they have sought to regain the spirit of the earlier rallies by reducing the advantages that the major well-funded teams enjoy. Their aim was to revive the adventure and regain the true amateur feeling of the event. They achieved this by plotting a new route that negated the knowledge of the terrain that regular competitors could use to their advantage. Further to this they introduced routes where navigation was by road book and compass, as it was in 1979 before the introduction of GPS. The 'Marathon' stages covering two days were without outside assistance which meant that the competitors had to maintain their own vehicles.

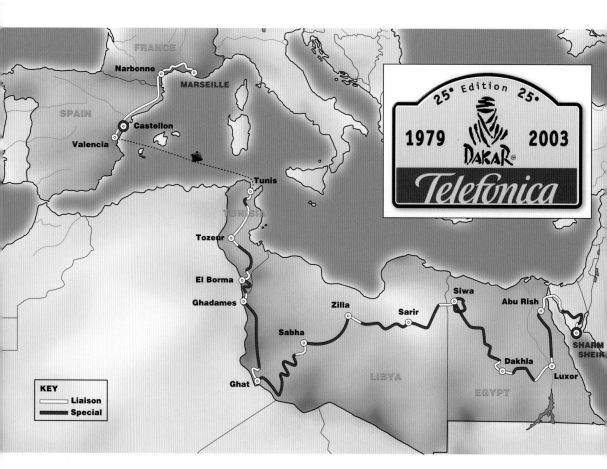

The European stages, from Marseille to Narbonne and on to Castellon and the port at Valencia, were straightforward. These early stages usually don't set the pattern for the rest of the event and the top competitors use them to settle in. After the Mediterranean crossing, traditionally used by the organisers for briefings and immigration documentation, the real competition begins.

The spectators cheer as Fabrizio Meoni, twice winner of the event, sets off on the Prologue on the big KTM

The Desert Warrior from RallyRaid UK team on the beach at Castellon, Spain

The harbour at Valencia

Last year's winner Meoni signs autographs at the end of the first special stage

Neville Murray from South Africa is interviewed by Eurosport

Leaving the special stage at Les Corbiers

Boarding the ferry for Africa

# Tunisia

The ferry docked early in the morning at La Goulette, the port of Tunis, and the competitors preceded south to the first African bivouac at Tozeur. Of the four hundred and sixty-three kilometres covered on this route only twenty-five was classed as a special stage. The following day saw the competitors making an early start in darkness and heading for El Borma. They covered a slightly longer route of which nearly three hundred kilometres was a special stage. On this stage they had their first experience of sand dunes and most of the hundred or so newcomers were relieved to have coped even though they knew there was worse to come. The villagers at the border crossing into Libya turned out to greet everyone and entertained them while they dealt with the customs formalities.

Entertainment by Tunisian children

Aqueduct

Welcome to Tunisia

LES HABITANTS DE BORJEL KHADRE
Remada   Eivine
SOUHAITENT BIENVENUE ET MEILLEURS
vœux pour tous
WELCOME
TO RALLYE PARIS-DAKAR IN TUNIS
BEST WISHES AND GOOD LUCK

# Libya

Competitors used the overnight stop at Ghadames to get as much sleep as possible as they knew that the following two-day 'Marathon' stage was going to test them to the limit. This had a combined length of over fourteen hundred kilometres, mostly gravel, sand and dunes. Assistance was not allowed at the overnight stop at Ghat; the competitors were on their own and had to service their own vehicles. The organisers expected over a third of the entry to fail on this long double stage. The top competitors seemed to take it in their stride but many of the amateurs suffered badly, especially the motorcyclists.

From Sabha the course moved on to Zilla and didn't offer any rest. The near six hundred kilometre stage was virtually all on gravel and sand, almost all of it was a special stage. The tired competitors still had two days before the rest day and along the route were some hard off-piste riding including a crossing of the Great Sand Sea. Then there was the overnight stop at Sarir followed the day after by the border crossing into Egypt.

Palmerie crops

Palmerie shack

Old village

Spectators near Murzuq in Libya

The local shop in Sabha

Entertainment by Libyan dancers

# Egypt

Rest at last for the competitors as they reached the oasis at Siwa where everyone was happy to settle down for two days at the same place. Mechanics were able to rebuild the bikes, cars, quads and trucks, while the competitors used the compulsory eighteen-hour rest period to shower and sleep. The next stage was a loop course, starting and finishing close to Siwa, which gave the assistance crew members a chance to see some of the real action. By this time the number of competitors was down by a third, not as low as the organisers had predicted.

Leaving Siwa the competitors headed back across the Great Sand Sea and through part of the Western Desert. This six hundred and fifty-seven kilometre stage was almost entirely off-piste with few tracks and required precise navigation. Many struggled throughout the night to arrive at the fabled oasis at Dakhla, knowing that the following day was rumoured to be easier. This journey to Luxor, although long at over seven hundred kilometres, was partly on tarmac and the off road part although sandy didn't include any dunes. There was however a steep ascent and descent on and off a plateau. Next morning the course was entering an increasingly higher populated part of Egypt as it headed north to Abu Rish. The Eastern Desert is mainly gravel with some sand and most of the competitors complained of the rough ride over the rocks.

By this stage everybody felt they were almost at the finish, Sharm El Sheikh had passed by just out of sight, on the other side of the Red Sea. The penultimate day, the longest at eight hundred and twenty-eight kilometres, meant a very early start at one o'clock in the

morning. In darkness the route was almost continuously passing through villages before reaching the tunnel under the Suez Canal. With the sparkling blue water of the Gulf of Suez on their right the competitors stayed on tarmac until they arrived at the start of the special stage. This long special on the Sinai Peninsula was to turn out to be a sting in the tail. The course twisted through high-sided canyons with plenty of loose rocks to catch the unwary. The rocky course twisted through tight climbs and many struggled to keep going. Those competitors who were contesting the lead were not exempt and in the car competition the lead changed twice before the day's result was declared. As Sharm El Sheikh filled up with support vehicles and competitors bikes, quads, cars and trucks, it was obvious that most competitors felt that the twenty-fifth Dakar was virtually finished. After all the final day was simply a short, thirty-four kilometre sprint for the benefit of the spectators.

A sprawling village alongside a canal in the Nile valley

31

Visiting the tombs near Siwa

Egypt customs post

Dovecote & Satellite Dish

## Sharm El Sheikh

The organisers were satisfied with the way this latest event had progressed with fifty newcomers arriving at the finish. They recognise that they still need innovative thinking to improve the event. In particular when 'bib-mouses' are considered, as these foam filled devices prevent punctures on motorcycles and have caused the speeds to increase. The result is that wheels are failing, with the top competitors using new wheels each day, a situation that penalises an amateur.

Sharm El Sheikh proved an excellent choice as a finishing location with modern hotels, bars, restaurants and clubs. After the harshness of the desert journey a party atmosphere soon developed as everyone enjoyed hot showers, sandy beaches, clear blue sea and the welcome of friends and family. Already discussions were taking place about next time and questions were being asked about the start and finish for the twenty-sixth 'Dakar'.

Czechs celebrate

Brazilians celebrate

Sinai Desert

# Taking part in the 'Dakar'

Decision, decisions, you have to make plenty of these before you can become involved in the event. Probably the earliest one concerns whether you will compete or be involved in some other way. There are four possibilities, you can enter as a competitor, work with an assistance team, report on the event as a journalist, or spectate.

While spectating may seem the easiest way and possibly a means of reconnoitring for later involvement it isn't as easy as it first appears. The 'Dakar' is impossible to follow along the entire route as every day the course travels through such a hostile

Press 'Landy'

VW assistance car

environment. Indeed, any attempt to keep up can be dangerous, as you need the sort of back-up services that are only provided by the organisers. These include fuel at out of the way places, medical services and repatriation by air if needed. However, it is possible to see the event at three places, the start, the rest day and the finish. The start is in Europe and easy to access by road or air, similarly the finish location can be easily visited. Any travel agent can find a short package holiday that bridges either the start or finish period and hiring a car will allow you to visit some of the stages. The official Dakar travel agency VSO organises a two or three day package to the rest day for

Motorcycle assistance team

Nissan mechanics at work

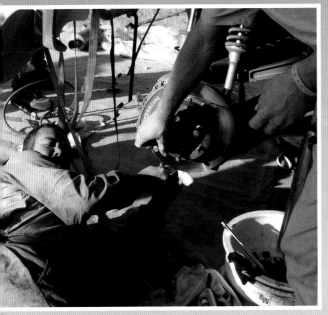

sponsors and mechanics. Visiting the rest day is the most interesting for any spectator as you can experience the evening bivouac and transport is arranged to take visitors to a special stage and to and from your hotel to the bivouac. Details are on the website.

If you have proven journalistic skills you may decide to report on the event and write about your experiences. This is probably the most difficult way of becoming involved with the 'Dakar'. You have to provide evidence that you have had work published for the last two years and that you hold a Press Card and have been commissioned to report on the event by at least one journal or agency. Once you have complied with these conditions you are then faced with a choice, you can travel in one of the organisers aircraft or you can drive yourself in a suitable vehicle. In this case suitable vehicle means a 4x4 that is virtually race specification. For obvious reasons the organisers limit the number of press cars and most journalists choose the plane package as the easiest solution. You will be flown to each bivouac, arriving early in the morning, in plenty of time to follow the progress of the competitors through the checkpoints and report on the news during the late afternoon.

Providing that you have the right skills you can offer your services as an assistance mechanic to a bike, car or truck team or individual competitor. Opportunities for this are sourced through the organisers but you have to make an early decision. You will pay an entry fee and be covered by all the support facilities. There will be some additional costs such as transport to the start and back home from the finish and hotel costs immediately before and after the event. During the event you will share all the facilities that the organisers provide and sleep in your tent at each bivouac. Every evening you will be expected to work on the vehicles until all the repairs and maintenance has been completed and try to get some sleep whenever there is an opportunity.

*Skiing superstar Luc Alphand and co-driver Matt Stevenson drive the BMW onto a special stage.*

The most exciting experience is as a competitor, either as a driver or co-driver, and the decision regarding the class of vehicle is an easy one. You will already know if you are a biker, quad racer, car driver or can handle a truck. Even those of us that are capable of competing in all these classes quickly find that cost becomes an important factor. As a co-driver in a car or truck you will be expected to share in some of the costs and all the information and details relating to entry fees and the entry forms can be downloaded from the organisers website. There then follows a long drawn out process of complying with various regulations covering licenses, vaccinations, visas, the hiring of safety equipment and working out the refuelling arrangements. By far the biggest task is ensuring that your chosen vehicle will comply with the complex regulations. There are ways of lessening the impact of these regulations and you will find them discussed later.

Spanish postman Mochales Garcia on his Honda 650

Antoine Morel driving a special Bombardier Quad

A big MAN truck driven by Phillipe Jaquot

## Giovani Sala

Giovani Sala as a young motorcyclist living in Bergamo in Northern Italy dreamed about riding in the Dakar rally. His first discipline was enduro and he concentrated on the World Championship series for many years as part of the strong KTM team. His success is without parallel and his riding skill and natural ability have earned him a place in the hall of fame of off road competitors. The rally team manager for KTM suggested that he try the Dubai Rally and Gio found an exciting experience that has now become his new passion. His first Dakar ride was in 1998 and he is now a regular member of the KTM team and finished in sixth place in 2002 riding the new twin cylinder LC8 Rallye. He has won many stages on the Dakar but won't commit himself to the suggestion that he could win the event, as he is very much a team member.

His advice to any newcomer is to join an experienced team and make their first attempt at the Dakar, as he did, as part racer and part tourist so that the adventure can be fully enjoyed.

Sala relaxes in his deluxe accommodation

## Vehicles

There are four categories of vehicles that can be used by competitors in the Dakar: motorcycle, quad, car or truck. Within these categories are different classes that regulate exactly the specification of your chosen vehicle.

For example, the car class has three separate groups. Group 1. is for 'Production' cross country cars which is further subdivided into Groups 1.1 & 1.2 for petrol and diesel engined types. This group conforms to the F.I.A. T1 Marathon class, a term that is usually used when referring to vehicles of this type. Next there is Group 2. which relates to 'Super Production' cross country cars, again this is subdivided. There are three classes, petrol & diesel engines are catered for along with a class for two wheel drive cars with either petrol or diesel engines. Included in this group are buggies and pro-trucks that conform

Emergency water tanks fitted low down into the motorcycle frame

Extra front light

to F.I.A. T2 specifications. All cars must have a height of less than two metres. Similar conditions exist for motorcycles, quads and trucks

Motorcycles and quads require extra lights at the front and rear of the machines, extra fuel tanks and an emergency water tank. A strong secure tool box is also essential as riders are not allowed to carry any tools on their person, either in pockets, waist bags or haversacks.

From the above you can see that even within your choice of vehicle there are further considerations that dictate which vehicle you choose and which class you will enter.

You can study these regulations by downloading the seventy-page document from the Dakar website. When you have sent your entry you will receive the same document in booklet form.

Emergency tanks fitted to the rear of a quad

Tyre inflator system

## Yoshimasa Sugawara

Japanese businessman Yoshimasa 'Yoshi' Sugawara has the rare distinction of being one of those competitors who has competed in the Dakar on a motorcycle, in a car and a truck. The 2003 event was his twenty-first Dakar and he achieved his seventeenth finish.
He didn't have much success on two wheels but the experience gained proved valuable when he drove a Mitsubishi Pajero and finished fifth in class. He found his niche in 1991 with the change to the truck class using a Hino Ranger. Since then he has won his class five times and never failed to finish. As the owner of Japan Racing Management he competes in many other desert rallies and his total is more than eighty events. At an age when most men would be thinking of retirement he continues with the commitment and enthusiasm of a young man.

Essential 'back-up' vehicle

Spare motorcycle wheels

Bikers boxes are transported by plane

## Costs

Competing in the Dakar can be expensive so it is important to make the right decisions. There are some expenses that are fixed; these include entry fees and hire of equipment. By carefully considering the others it is possible to save money, such as on the cost of a vehicle, spare parts and service.

The entry fees are charged 'per person' so that you pay for one on a motorcycle or quad, two in a car and three in a truck. Equipment hire covers an emergency beacon and the official GPS, which all competitors have to use. To hire these items you pay a fixed cost and a refundable deposit that is returned after the event finishes, provided the items have been handed back in good condition. Whichever class you enter you will need to provide yourself with suitable clothing and an approved helmet. Generally motorcyclists and quad drivers will need to spend more on race clothing than car or truck competitors.

By far the biggest cost will be the provision of a vehicle. You can use a second-hand one provided you feel it will be reliable and meets the regulations. There are some trail motorcycles, such as the Honda 650, that can be quickly and economically brought up to rally specification, similarly there are standard 4x4's that can be treated in the same way. If you have sufficient funds you can buy a race ready KTM 660, a fully prepared 4x4 or a special space-frame car. For the truck class the problems are not only larger they tend to be more expensive.

Having made the major decision about your vehicle there are four items that have to be arranged: spare parts, tyres, fuel and assistance. Motorcycle competitors are provided with a large metal box for their parts, which along with two spare wheels is transported for them by aircraft to each bivouac. Any additional items and tyres they, like the car competitors, have to pay a service organisation to carry them in one of their trucks. Whatever vehicle you use it may be possible to obtain spare parts on a sale or return basis which can save a lot of expense.

On some parts of the route, especially in mainland Europe, fuel is available at roadside petrol stations. At other places the organisation provide a refuelling service and all car and truck competitors have to forecast their needs and order and pay for the fuel in advance. The fuel for motorcycle competitors is paid for with the entry fee and refuelling points are organised where needed.

Service and assistance is one aspect of the Dakar that requires serious thought as trying to compete and look after your vehicle yourself isn't the best way. After a long day on the course you will be tired and hungry and still have to carry out routine work or major repairs. Important problems are often missed or not dealt with thoroughly, sleep is lost and the next day is a disaster. The alternatives are that you pay for the use of a mechanic on a support truck or alternatively for your own mechanic to travel with a support team. Probably the best solution to seriously consider is to pay for a total package that includes motorcycle or car hire, spare parts, and the services of a mechanic. This is referred to as a 'turnkey' package and can often work out cheaper than trying to organise everything for yourself. There is one British and several continental organisations offering this kind of service package and there is more on this subject later.

French car and assistance truck

Dutch Jaguar with assistance car

# Finding the money

Everybody who competes in the Dakar is sponsored in one way or another. It is worth taking a quick look at the dictionary definition so that you understand the meaning fully. As a competitor improves, the level of sponsorship improves to the point when as a professional rider or driver all the costs are covered.

As a newcomer it is worth fixing the idea in your head that unless somebody will sponsor you the full cost will have to come from your own funds.

The methods of obtaining sponsorship and the type or degree of support vary so much that it is difficult to clearly define. There are however some guidelines that are worth remembering.

You should always talk to potential sponsors about what you will be 'doing for them'. Never slip into the habit of just asking for the money or they will assume your main interest is in enjoying yourself at their expense. Keep in mind that the person you are talking to will not know anything about the Dakar, even if they say otherwise. The TV coverage that they may have watched reports on the leaders and the winning positions. Present a folder with relevant material about the event, the media coverage and state clearly what benefits they can expect. As a newcomer you cannot expect to win the event and you should make this clear. Everybody can offer an enthusiastic approach to generating publicity, via local media etc, but only offer that which is achievable. Never forget that during and after the event you will need to report on your progress.

The official vehicle numbers for the Dakar have exact positions on the vehicles where they must be placed and for motorcyclists the numbered patches cover a large part of the front and rear area of the riders' jacket. Work out a schematic of your vehicle, race wear and paddock clothing and allocate space for sponsors names and/or logos, stating clearly in advance where these can be positioned. As a rule side images of the vehicle are best but remember that clothing such as helmets and overalls is often seen in close up. Motorcyclists have the most difficult problem due to the lack of space on the machine but they do however have the space on their clothing with the arms, legs and kneecaps being the prime areas.

Often it is tempting to wait and see what you are offered but the correct approach is to decide on a budget. This involves some early decisions based on your total cost of competing. Should you look for one sponsor to pay the whole cost and risk having nothing if you fail, or go for many sponsors and have more work finding them? With the latter you have some security should you only find say nine out of the ten you were seeking. Alternatively should you seek a main sponsor and a number of smaller sponsors? At the 2003 Dakar one motorcyclist had three thousand sponsors each contributing ten pounds. He had spent four months selling enamel badges to friends, neighbours, work-mates and strangers.

Always write to confirm the sponsorship and include a stage payment plan that calls for part of the money to be paid immediately followed by the balance on a certain date. This helps you to meet your early commitments and also insures that the sponsors are aware when funds are required. Most potential sponsors will recognise this as a responsible approach.

As soon as a sponsor accepts your offer to promote his company or product, and that is the correct phrase, immediately visit all your local newspapers and ring your local radio stations. They are always searching for news about a local company and they will be interested in your plans. When you have finalised all the funding prepare a press release with a photograph and send it to the trade journals that cover all your sponsors' trades. The addresses are at the local library.

Offer to meet with your sponsors for a pre-event photo shoot so they can see your vehicle and clothing complete with their company name or logo. Finally, when you return home from the event you should revisit your sponsors and thank them personally. Use this occasion to give them a signed, framed action photo of yourself complete with Dakar logo and any other souvenirs of the event. All the costs of this hospitality will of course been included in your original budget.

## Support

Many competitors fail to pay enough attention to this aspect assuming that it will all fall into place. Crossing their fingers they hope they don't have a major problem only to find that when they do it becomes obvious that any savings they have made may have cost them heavily. Saving money on support that later causes your retirement isn't sensible.

There are a number of options and the worst is not making any arrangements for service and support. Attempting to carry out all the work on your vehicle by yourself, or with the help of co-drivers, is usually unsuccessful.

A better option is to sign up with an organisation who can provide all the support services, including a team of skilled mechanics each evening at the bivouac. The truck will carry all the necessary equipment, lights, generator, an air line and your boxes of spare parts and a welcoming service area will be waiting for you at the end of each day. More importantly the truck or 4x4 fast assistance car will be out there at the designated assistance points along the course ready to help and support you during the event. One company that can offer this level of support is RallyRaid UK using well equipped six wheel drive trucks and 4x4 cars. When you arrive at a bivouac you hand your bike or car over to the service manager and tell him clearly what needs doing. You can relax, get some food and rest before marking up the road-book for next day and attending the evening briefing. If your motorcycle or car is seriously damaged they will, if need be, work throughout the night so that it is ready for you next day. This happens frequently and it is worth thinking about how you would manage if you tried to do this yourself.

Another option is to find the money for a complete package that offers all the above support and service along with the rental of a suitable vehicle. RallyRaid UK offers these types of packages but an early decision is needed, as they cannot produce a vehicle for you at the last minute. If you decide to compete on a motorcycle you can choose between a Honda XR650 and a KTM 660 Rallye. The package for the former is not so expensive,

while the KTM package includes a factory prepared machine. For car competitors RallyRaid UK produce their own BMW powered space frame racer that is far better than a converted road going 4x4. The benefits of a complete package begin before you even arrive at the start as they deal with entries, equipment hire, fuel arrangements, spare parts and tyres. The motorcycle or car will have been carefully prepared so you can be confident that it will satisfy the scrutineer's requirements. The team manager will guide you through the maze of documentation and already have arranged for your team clothing. The team members will work hard before and during the event to make sure that you arrive safely at the finish.

By taking this option you will have provided yourself with the best support that you can afford. The surprise is that, due to their expertise in organising this type of assistance, it will cost you very little more than doing everything by yourself. You can arrive at the start, join a friendly team and then concentrate on enjoying the adventure.

Newcomer Britains Nick Plumb rode his BMW through sand and big rocks
finding reserves of strength and with sheer determination reached the finish

Spanish rider Jose Luis Alvarez dominates his Bombardier quad

Britain's Paul Round from Huddersfield is a four times Dakar competitor. His experiences as a first timer with his son Mark without any support or assistance made him realise that it is essential to be part of a team to achieve any kind of success. The difficulties he encountered in dealing with the French officials before and during the rally caused him the most problems, as information is a very important element. In 2001, working with Andrew Neri, he set up RallyRaid UK a support organisation with the sole aim of helping other English-speaking competitors. This service and assistance organisation has helped and encouraged many motorcycle and car competitors to take part in the Dakar and other desert rallies. RallyRaid UK also builds the space framed, Desert Warrior race cars, equipped with BMW diesel engines and prepares Honda and KTM rally motorcycles. Drivers and riders can choose from a variety of packages to suit their exact requirements and even arrange for their

Paul & Neville Murray

Rebuilding motorcycle on rest day (no engine)

own mechanic to be part of the team. Competitors can either rent or provide their own vehicle and have the services of skilled mechanics and an experienced team manager to assist them through most of the organisational problems.

# Documents & Visas

During the registration process, at the start, you will be required to provide certain documents. These include vehicle registration forms and a letter authorising you to use it, if you are not the owner. You will also need a copy of your insurance certificate that specifically relates to the vehicle you will use. These documents must be originals, photocopies are not accepted. You may also be required to show a vaccination certificate indicating that you have complied with the organiser's list of injections.

Your passport should have at least six months before it needs renewal and have valid visas for the countries that the event passes through. Some countries in North Africa require that you send your passport to their Paris office and it can be in their hands for a long time. If you intend to leave your own country during this period for a holiday or on business you would be well advised to apply for a duplicate passport as early as possible.

Competitors have to apply for and pay for all their visas and a list is provided which shows the requirements for all nationalities. Application forms can be downloaded or obtained from the organisers by post and should be completed and sent off well in advance of the event. Do not leave this to the last minute as non Europeans may find it is impossible to gain entry to Europe if they do not have their passport.

Other documents may be required during the signing-on process so it is important to study the instructions that the organisers send to you when you enter the event.

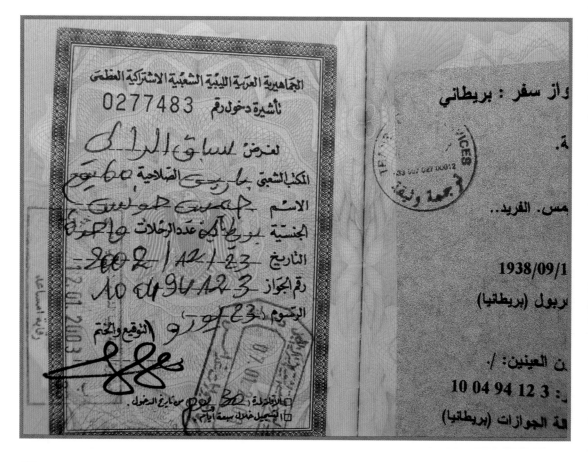

# Safety equipment

A lot of the organiser's effort is used on ensuring the safety of everybody involved in the event. Certain requirements have to be complied with and are checked during scrutineering and possibly at other times. Obvious ones concern a competition or an assistance vehicle's ability to communicate that they are in trouble. All competitors' vehicles are fitted with an emergency beacon that acts as a locater for the emergency helicopters. The beacons are rented from the organisers and once activated the competitor has retired from the event. This means that after pushing the button you cannot change your mind and continue. Assistance vehicles do not carry a beacon but have a satellite telephone, the same type as all the competitors, and can be used in an emergency.

The list of smaller safety items is long and includes the following. A cigarette lighter, for setting fire to a tyre for use as a distress beacon, a strobe light, a torch and three smoke flares. More obvious ones are a compass, distress mirror, survival blankets, powerful horns and, for cars, a seat belt cutter. All vehicles have to carry five litres of water per person in addition to any drinking water also carried. Cars and trucks should carry a tent, sleeping bags and emergency supplies in case they have to stay out on the course overnight.

Failure to carry any of the above items can result in immediate exclusion from the event and/or financial penalties. This is an indication of how seriously the organisers take your safety and how serious the consequences are of disregarding the dangers of the desert.

You don't get a second chance in the desert

Numbers are attached to a Volvo

## Signing on and scrutineering

You will often hear competitors saying that it can be as difficult getting to the start of the Dakar as it is getting to the finish. This is not true, but it does indicate how seriously the organisers study your paperwork and every part of your vehicle. Of course, everybody knows that this is a good thing and is well intentioned but the tension shows on the faces of many competitors when they start this process. They know that they can be sent back for either major or minor reasons. Major means that the vehicle doesn't conform to the regulations and cannot compete. Minor means some small thing, such as the size of the rear lights is wrong and that they can be corrected. This is where a complete package from an organisation such as RallyRaid UK helps to remove the stress that individuals, particularly newcomers, suffer. RallyRaid use their experience and devote time to studying and conforming to new regulations so that they can avoid these problems.

To ensure that you do not miss any part of the process all competitors are given a yellow form with their photograph attached. You start by submitting your documents to various officials and as you move from counter to counter the boxes are ticked as you deal with the medics, safety equipment, fuel and many other things. Once all the personal details are completed you are allowed to bring your vehicle into the scrutineers hall where yet more boxes are ticked off.

The officials start by checking the class that the vehicle has been entered in and that it conforms to the correct specification. An example of this is the air intake size for the capacity of engine that is fitted to a car or motorcycle. For this a restrictor plate has to be fitted in a way that it cannot be removed or bypassed. Once happy with the arrangement they wire and lead seal it into place. There are many conditions in all classes similar to this example that have to be complied with.

When they are satisfied that the car or motorcycle conforms to its entry class they move on to the details of the vehicle and whether it is assembled properly. At all times during this inspection the competitors must remain with the vehicle so that they can answer queries.

The Desert Warrior is subjected to a thorough examination

Riders jacket has number bib securely attached

The officials are looking for unsafe or illegal construction of any part of the vehicle.

Having satisfied these requirements you are instructed to move to the section where the Dakar plates and other stickers are attached. Only now do you feel that you are making progress. It is short lived; you still face a detailed check of your safety equipment and a helmet check. Motorcyclists wear a helmet at all times, but all other competitors and assistance crews have to carry an FIA approved helmet that they must wear on all the special stages and on off-road sections of the route.

Spare wheels are carried in special frames at the rear of the car

The final check is the yellow form itself; every box must be ticked and stamped. Only then can you emerge from the scrutineering hall and allow yourself a sigh of relief, as the whole process will have taken hours. Competitors cars have a brief period before they must be placed in the 'parc ferme', and at this stage you know your Dakar has begun because the spectators are already asking you for your autograph.

Checking the safety items on board the Yamaha quad

# Derrick Edmondson

Derrick is one of Britain's best known off-road competitors. His riding career started in 1976 and by 1983 he had won his first British Enduro championship, the first of nine class and overall wins. In those days, before the World series was inaugurated, Derrick finished runner-up to Frenchman Gilles Lalay in the European Championship.

Alongside his reputation as a rider he has earned similar status in every other facet of the sport. As a mechanic he worked with many top trials and enduro riders including World Trials champion Eddie Lejuerne during his HRC days. Later with Cagiva he was involved with the Lucky Explorer team that included Danny Laporte, Eddie Orioli and other great riders. That was the year of the Paris-Le Cap Rallye when Derrick drove a team Unimog in the event, his first involvement with the Dakar. In 2003 Derek returned to the Dakar and rode a KTM to a creditable placing. Now a successful motorcycle dealer his ambition is to compete in a car and join that select band of competitors who have arrived at the finish on a bike, in a car and in a truck.

Derrick about to be overtaken and covered in dust

Derrick and Mick shake hands at the finish

## Mick Extance

Englishman Mick Extance from Derby is a successful enduro rider who has recently discovered the excitement of desert rallying. Following a win in the British Enduro Championship and a high finish in the World Series he won the European Veterans Enduro Championship. After a brief spell at Downhill Mountain bike events, which included winning a British Championship, he decided to make a three-year commitment to the Dakar in order to assess his long-term future in desert rallying.

He rode in the 2002 Dakar as a RallyRaid team member but an unfortunate electrical fire on his machine forced his retirement. When he rode onto the finishing podium at the end of the 2003 event he was ecstatic and immediately began preparations for next year with the aim of a higher finishing position. He was quick to thank all the RallyRaid mechanics and support crew who had worked tirelessly to keep both man and machine in full working order throughout the event.

Mick at the start of special stage in Sinai

Mick at the finish

# Full colour road book

During signing on every participant is given a small full colour road book that contains detailed information about the entire route, a list of competitors and officials. The pages contain a detailed map, start and finish times, length of the route in kilometres, time allowed, brief description of the area and a cross section of the terrain for every day. This full colour road book is a most useful item and should be kept close at hand throughout the event.

These examples from an actual road book illustrate the information about the first marathon stage. This marathon stage, without any assistance, from Ghadames to Ghat in Libya had a liaison stage of 5km to the start of the 584km special stage. Then a final 102kms liaison stage to the bivouac added up to a day's total of 691kms with a maximum time allowance of 14 hours. The first motorcyclist will leave the start of the special stage at 8.15am and will be expected at the final control in Ghat at 3.30pm. Another page from the road book shows a cross section of the terrain for this route and an indication of where the control points, fuel and a dangerous descent are positioned.

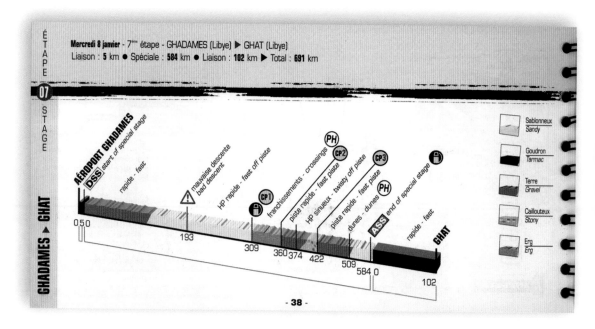

# Daily road book

The daily road book contains a graphical method of showing the route that all competitors or assistance vehicles must follow. The display is called 'ball & arrow', and the direction of travel is from the 'ball' to the 'arrow'. When you reach the 'arrow' you go to the next instruction box. To the left of each diagram there is a box showing two figures and the larger is the total distance travelled. The second figure indicates the distance from the 'ball'

Checking the road book

to the 'arrow', in other words the distance that you should travel before moving onto the next instruction box. To the right of the diagram there are abbreviations that give information about landmarks or dangerous terrain where you should exercise caution. These abbreviations tell the navigator what the diagram is depicting and are relative to French so a translation is provided at the front of the road book.

The road book provided for the motorcyclists and quad riders is in the form of a roll that is attached onto rollers in a special holder mounted on the handlebars. The current instruction is kept between two black lines on the transparent cover of the road book holder. One button on the handlebars allows the rider to move the road book one instruction at a time and resets the trip meter to zero. Another button on the left-hand bar will reverse the roller. The rider will take note of the distance on the road book and wait for that number to appear on his trip meter. At that point the next landmark as shown on his road book should appear and the process is repeated.

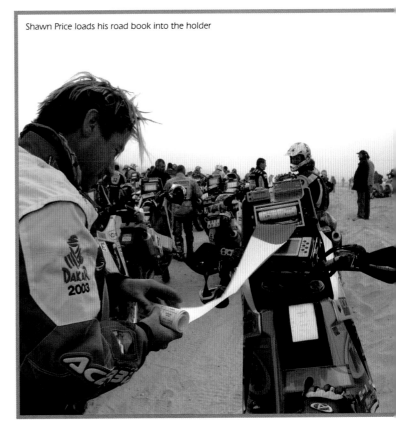

Shawn Price loads his road book into the holder

The road book for car and truck competitors is in the form of a book and as each landmark is passed the navigator will strike out each instruction. A good tip with this type of road book is just before reaching the last instruction of a page to check over the next page for the distance to the first landmark. If this distance is short say 0.40 kms or 400 metres the driver can be given the change of direction in good time.

Looking at page 30 of the road book the competitor can see that part of the route covering just 6.50 kms through sand dunes will require five changes of direction. Following the compass headings will take the route close to the border with Algeria, indicted by a frontier marker and a big cairn.

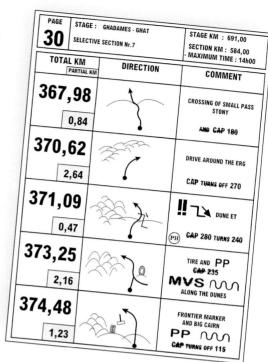

| PAGE 30 | STAGE : GHADAMES - GHAT | STAGE KM : 691,00 |
|---|---|---|
| | SELECTIVE SECTION Nr.7 | SECTION KM : 584,00 MAXIMUM TIME : 14h00 |

| TOTAL KM PARTIAL KM | DIRECTION | COMMENT |
|---|---|---|
| **367,98** 0,84 | | CROSSING OF SMALL PASS STONY AND CAP 180 |
| **370,62** 2,64 | | DRIVE AROUND THE ERG CAP TURNS OFF 270 |
| **371,09** 0,47 | | ‼ DUNE ET PH CAP 280 TURNS 240 |
| **373,25** 2,16 | | TIRE AND PP CAP 235 MVS ALONG THE DUNES |
| **374,48** 1,23 | | FRONTIER MARKER AND BIG CAIRN PP CAP TURNS OFF 115 |

Patsy Quick and Mick Extance concentrate on highlighting their road book for the next day

The second picture of the daily road book is a section of the circular special stage that started and finished just outside Siwa. The total distance is 445 kms and a maximum time allowance of eleven hours. The two pages, 16 and 17, show how important it is to keep a watchful eye on the next following instruction over the page. At a distance of just 600 metres is a warning for another downhill step and a driver would not want to arrive there without any warning. Also indicted is a GPS reading for control point 3 where motorcycles will be refuelled and assistance is authorised for all competitors.

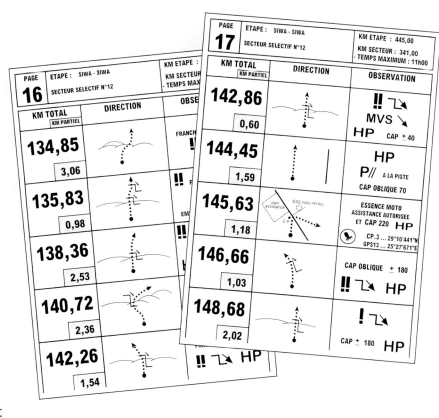

It is usual for a competitor to mark the road book each evening and coloured highlighter pens are ideal for this purpose. One colour is used to highlight the direction of travel, another colour for dangerous terrain and another for compass headings.

Group of drivers trying to find the best route through the soft sand

## G.P.S. (Global Positioning Satellite)

Desert markers are difficult to see in the sand

The GPS system is a navigation aid that covers the entire surface of the earth. Used correctly it can tell you exactly where you are, which direction you need to go in to reach an exact point, your speed over the ground and record the distance to travel. The type of equipment used by competitors in the Dakar is more sophisticated than most and is provided to all competitors by the organisation in advance with some of the functions disabled. Supplied complete with all the brackets and leads that connect to your vehicle, these are charged for but the detachable GPS unit is rented from the organisation and it is the sole responsibility of the competitor to make sure the unit is secure. The GPS is mounted above the headstock on motorcycles and quads directly in front of the rider while in cars and trucks it is placed in front of the co-driver. Because the driver will often need to drive on a certain compass heading a repeater is supplied for mounting within his line of sight. Many car drivers will want to use two GPS units just in case one should become faulty.

The full route for the event from the start to the final finishing point is already stored in the GPS memory but to prevent any prior knowledge of the route you cannot access this information. Before the start of each day an access code is announced and when this is entered into the GPS that day's route is displayed. The use of any other extra form of navigational aid such as a laptop or mobile phone with GPS is strictly forbidden and violation will mean instant exclusion.

The GPS is used in conjunction with the daily road book that is supplied each night at the final control. The GPS, where appropriate to the road book instruction, displays an arrow that indicates the direction you should take to the next 'way-point'. It also tells you how far that

Drivers briefing about safety and navigation

GPS and road book holder fixed behind the motorcycle fairing

GPS and distance trip meter are positioned in front of the co-driver

point is from your present position. The 'way-point' is a latitude and longitude position and when reached the GPS tells you which way to go to the next location. Some parts of the course are not marked by a 'way-point' but are found by following a compass heading. The GPS displays a direction arrow that points you in the right direction. These compass directions have to be followed 'intelligently', on some occasions on totally flat desert you can travel in a straight line. On others you have to weave around dunes or rock outcrops and you must strive to cancel out these variations.

There is another feature of the GPS that will not concern most competitors unless you go in for some serious course cutting. In the desert the actual course may be several kilometres wide and the organisers accept this, by making clever use of the road book and the GPS it is possible to cut the course. If the organisers suspect that you have done this deliberately they can replay your actual course and check it out. If they find that you have been more than eleven kilometres off course you can incur a time penalty. Frequently a competitor, if genuinely lost, can be a long way off course and the organisers can tell that he hasn't benefited from this deviation and do not impose a penalty.

On the days when all the navigation has to be without the aid of the GPS the competitors are given two codes. The first will only activate the compass screen and this is all that is allowed. Should a competitor become lost or have an emergency then the second code will activate the equipment as normal but a time penalty will be imposed.

Any first time competitors who are not familiar with the workings of the GPS navigation system would benefit from studying the subject. Do not concern yourself too much with the different types of equipment as full information is provided by the organisation and on the ferry crossing briefings, in several languages, are held to instruct everyone how to use the equipment.

# Distance trip meter

Motorcycle and quad riders have a trip meter, positioned behind the front fairing, that shows a display of distance travelled. This meter has to be calibrated and can be reset from a switch on the handlebars at each turning point or landmark shown on the road book. Cars and trucks are fitted with one or two special trip meters, which once calibrated can give the co-driver more information about distances, speed and time.

The 'Terratrip' is one make of unit that is in effect the equivalent of the odometer and trip on a speedometer. Usually mounted in front of the co-driver, next to the GPS, the liquid crystal display will show either the total distance travelled each day, which is only reset each morning or the intermediate distance at each instruction on the road book. As a point is reached, identified by some feature or GPS reading on the road book, the co-driver strikes out that instruction and will reset the trip. The co-driver must then watch for the next distance shown on the road book to be displayed on the display when the correct landmark should be visible. All distances are in kilometres and it can be helpful for competitors more used to miles to try and get experience of the shorter measurements.

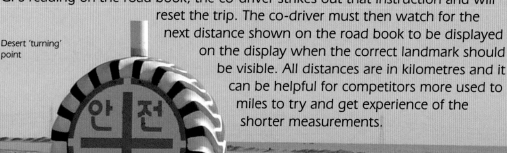

Desert 'turning' point

Libyan achievement

Oil drums mark the way

The three components of the navigation system are therefore, the road book, the GPS unit and the trip meter or the distance indicator for motorcyclists. Used together in conjunction with compass headings these items will tell the competitor in which direction to travel and how far it is to the next turning point or landmark. Used correctly these enable you to find your way through any terrain but it is still very easy to lose concentration and miss a landmark or turning point. Realising you are lost can sometimes be difficult and competitors have been known to make the road book instructions 'fit' the terrain rather than retrace the route to the last known correct point.

Occasionally competitors will follow tracks in the sand with no other vehicles in sight and ignore the road book instructions. Tracks in the sand can be used only to confirm that you are following a route that other vehicles have used. On seeing another vehicle ahead some competitors will take the easy option and just follow assuming that the leading vehicle is on the correct route. Meanwhile the competitor in the leading vehicle is reassured by the presence of the following ones assuming that they know where they are. This method of navigation can result in a group of competitors becoming lost and travelling a long way in the wrong direction. It is important to have confidence in your navigation skills and to make your own decisions about the direction of the course based on the facts presented by those three components.

Every town has a unique gateway

Road signs are unusual

# Women competitors

Many Dakar enthusiasts regard the event as a male preserve. Despite this, over the years, many women have taken part. The twenty-fifth anniversary event was no exception, there were ten ladies competing. This shouldn't be taken as minor involvement because without female input the event would probably grind to a stop. There are many ladies working, both at the head office and the bivouac, who do clerical, medical and support work.

There were two experienced lady drivers, Jutta Kleinshmidt who won the event in 2001 and Andrea Mayer who was previously a highly placed motorcyclist. The former chose Fabrizia Pons as her co-driver and five male drivers also chose lady co-drivers. Elizabeth Jacinto, who had previously competed on a motorcycle, switched to driving a truck, the only lady competitor in that class. In the motorcycle class there were two female riders, Frenchwoman Astrid Pichegrain rode a KTM 660 and won the Ladies class while Briton Patsy Quick chose to ride a Honda 650.

Patsy, a Dakar newcomer, is a former British Ladies Enduro Champion and won the European Ladies Enduro Championship in 2001 at her first attempt. Riding in the 1998 Optic Tunisia Rally she was the first British lady to finish a desert rally. Her first Dakar came to an abrupt end in Egypt when a heavy fall resulted in hospital treatment. Patsy explained how important it is to understand the navigation system before starting in the event. While riding the motorcycle across unknown territory and across rough terrain it is sometimes difficult to keep moving while trying to follow the road book instructions, read the GPS screen and watch the trip meter. Patsy would often stop to check her exact position as a lot of time and energy is wasted if a turning point is missed. Navigating through the dunes in the darkness is an extra hazard as often the landmark can be just out of the range of the headlights so Patsy tried to make sure that she completed the special stages before darkness fell.

Andrea Mayer chooses four wheels rather than her usual two and drives through the water splash

Elodie Metge and her father Rene, a former winner, make a great team

Newcomer Astrid Pichegrain rode her KTM to the finish and collected the Ladies prize

## Daily route

Throughout the event each day follows a similar pattern with the road book instructions starting from the bivouac control point. Assistance vehicles can leave at anytime but the co-driver must collect a time card to record the departure from the bivouac and this card must be handed in upon arrival at the finish control. Competitors are given a starting time for each day based on their finishing position on the previous day's special stage. Half an a hour before that starting time competitors must present themselves and their vehicle at the control point where they will be given a time card for that day. If there is a long liaison section there will be a time allowance, which gives a reasonable time to travel to the start of the special stage. Radar speed traps may be set up in the villages along this route and all vehicles travelling too fast or in an

Patrick Zaniroli reaches for the time card

unsafe manner will be penalised. Along the liaison route assistance from mechanics may be allowed and service crews will be parked at a location indicated in the road book.

The special stage will start and finish at a control point, where the time card is stamped and the exact time each competitor crossed the start and finish line is recorded and transmitted to rally control headquarters. Along the special stage there are more control points where it is the responsibility of all competitors to make sure their time card is stamped. The passage of competitors through these control points is also relayed to rally control. Should a competitor miss a control point along the route the vehicle GPS will be checked to verify the route taken and a penalty will be imposed. There is a specified distance, usually eleven kilometers, that vehicles can be away from the official route before being penalised.

The time taken on the special stage is added onto the previous day's totals and the time accumulates throughout the event. The only exception is the prologue when the time taken is used only to determine the starting times for the next day.

Typical end of 'special' stage

Early morning desert start

Long day at a time control

Added to the running total will be any time penalties imposed by the stewards for late arrival or other infractions of the rules.

Places along the special stages where assistance by mechanics is permitted are shown in the road book and all the time taken is included in the total stage time. The only neutral time zones are for motorcycle refuelling. Any other help along the special stage must come from fellow competitors. There will be another time allowance for the liaison route from the end of the special stage to the final control and assistance may be allowed at a designated location.

At the final control point, usually at the entrance to the bivouac, the time card will be collected and the road book for next day will be available. If a competitor arrives at a control point after the time allowed a penalty is given and they must make their arrival at the bivouac and the reason for the delay known to the organisers. If they suspect any diversion from the route the GPS may be checked and further time penalties imposed.

Arriving very late at the final control of the day doesn't mean automatic exclusion. Competitors who have been lost or had a mechanical breakdown frequently decide to sleep out in the desert and will continue in daylight and arrive in time for breakfast. Provided they present themselves and the vehicle at the start control point at their due time, that is thirty minutes before their start time, they can usually continue with the event. If they only just manage this deadline it is sometimes possible to double back to the bivouac for fuel, food and even repairs. Late starting may result in extra penalties especially if they miss their start time at the special stage.

Japanese champion, Jun Matsuhashi, looks relaxed

New friends Shawn Price (US) & Jose Luis Steuri (Esp)

Have my water –
Phillipe Gauthier &
Elodie Metge

Paul Round & Jim Jones listen to Ari Vatanen

Out in the desert Richard Sainct rides his KTM with skill and finesse

Mick Extance powers his Honda 650 through a special stage

French Land Rover Discovery driven by Yannick Commagnac and Yves Coquelin

Fuel for the machine – water for the rider

Relaxing on the luxurious carpets in the cafeteria

The sand sticks to everything

Phillipe Gauthier endures a dusting down by Gilles his mechanic

The washing dries quickly in the hot sunshine

# Bivouac

The successful organisation of the desert bivouacs is vital to the smooth running of the rally. Every day the organisers use a fleet of transport aircraft to move all the equipment and paraphernalia to the next location. Usually on the side of an airfield they set up 'shop' under the wings of the aircraft. With plenty of available space they organise the medical facility, press room and communication facility. Local service crews will already have erected the cafeteria tents and provided water tankers and fuel supplies. Apart from service and support facilities, the bivouac provides food, water, shelter, communication, information and help of every kind. It does not however offer luxuries such as showers and similar comforts. Everybody sleeps in a tent close to the vehicles and has to ignore the noise and any discomforts, which is part of the challenge that makes the Dakar special.

The day starts before dawn for the bivouac team as everything is packed up ready to be moved hundreds of miles to where they do it all again. Perhaps they are the 'heroes' of the event.

For everybody involved whether they are competitors, assistance, press or officials, the bivouac is their 'family home' for the night. As the event progresses the friendly atmosphere intensifies as team spirit builds confidence and shared experiences develop into new friendships.

There is time for a relaxing game

Fresh local vegetables for sale

The packed lunch is full of high energy snacks

# Food

While the event is in Europe everyone is responsible for feeding themselves and it is only after reaching Africa that the bivouacs take the place of hotels for overnight accommodation.

When arriving at a bivouac your first consideration will be vehicle maintenance and food. The cafeteria will be there waiting for you and during the afternoon you will find hot and cold drinks and snacks are available. On the noticeboard will be the time of the evening meal and the menu, which is European style food. The catering staff will prepare a nourishing meal for over a thousand persons with soup, main course and dessert and a choice of drinks including wine and beer is on offer. Around the food area is a tented and carpeted Arab style encampment where you dine by sitting cross-legged on the floor. Early next morning there is a buffet style breakfast of cereals, cold ham, fried eggs, yoghurts and hot coffee, tea or chocolate.

Drinking lots of bottled water is essential

A campsite under the wing on the airfield

Immediately after breakfast you collect a packed lunch and bottled water. The lunches are the same each day and are designed as high-energy food and not necessarily as a gourmet snack. Nuts, energy bars, meat sticks, cheese and toasted bread and biscuits form the basis of these packs along with cartons of fruit purée, dried prunes and fruit juice. Most people do not like everything and will supplement the rations with fresh bread and jam collected at breakfast. The motorcyclists will take the items they like and fill their pockets while the car occupants will sort out their preferences as they drive. If possible everyone should build up an emergency supply of items for use when the cafeteria is closed. Water is very important and you must take your supply of bottled water every morning.

Luxurious dining room

Fried eggs anyone?

Enjoying an early morning breakfast

## Information

Information about the event is important to everyone and there are two noticeboards at the bivouac. The main board is positioned close to the organisers office which is usually adjacent to the aeroplane parking area and the second board is at the cafeteria close to the food counters. Both boards will display an assortment of notices concerning the news, route changes, penalties imposed by the stewards, copies of press releases, team events and the latest results. The latest available results will show the time and date and will be progressive as competitors pass through the checkpoints. The final results for the day's stage and overall positions will remain on the board until the next day. Most teams and service organisations have press officers who will collect all this information for the benefit of the team managers and service crews.

The most important information concerns the next day's route, the changes to the road book as reported by the course openers, the hazards that the organisers want to highlight and the code for the GPS. Each evening around eight o'clock a briefing is held at the giant TV screen in the cafeteria where everyone will gather to watch the outgoing television coverage of the event. Although the commentary and briefing are in French, personal earphones with translations into different languages are provided.

Studying the noticeboard at the bivouac

A copy of the day's results is interesting reading material

Team manager Andrew Neri (second from right) holds a lunch time meeting with the team mechanics

Gerard Barbezant does his morning warming up exercises which helped him ride his KTM 125cc all the way to the finish

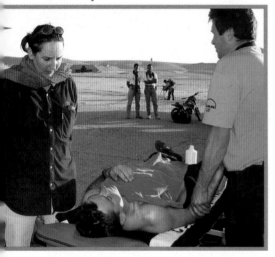

When is it my turn?

That was a very hard drive

## Fatigue management

While most competitors worry about their vehicle lasting the distance many don't give the same thought to their bodies, assuming they are fit enough to last whatever happens. The problem of fatigue is accumulative and as the day's progress and the course becomes more technical fatigue takes its toll.

Many competitors blame a lack of concentration or bad luck when they fall off a motorcycle or roll a car. In most cases the competitor was too tired to perform at his best and this is worse for newcomers and amateurs. The leading competitors reach the bivouac early in the day and will retire to their tents while others are out on the course longer, sometimes as long as three or four hours. Then they are involved with the maintenance of their vehicle and will get less than half the sleep of the leading competitors. Ten days later they are seriously under performing and begin to understand the advantage of having a good service and assistance package.

This is where 'Fatigue Management' is so important and the simplest analogy is to compare your energy to a battery. You do not want to arrive at the start of the event with a flat battery so you need to get plenty of rest before you leave home. You will use energy during each day and recharge it at night with the aim of completely replacing what you have used. If this isn't possible the battery charge is slowly descending to the inevitable day when the battery is completely discharged. It is the same with your body, replace energy at every possible moment. Co-drivers can take their turn at the wheel on the long liaison sections allowing the driver to rest and be fresher for the special stage. Motorcycle and quad riders should try to rest when they arrive at the start of the special test or along the liaison route at a café or fuel stop. Don't walk around if you don't need to, find a comfy place, stretch out and watch everybody else wasting energy.

Think about 'Fatigue Management' all the time.

## Medical

The comprehensive medical services throughout the event, both out on the course and at the bivouac, are provided by a French company called Fidelia Assurance. During signing on you must register with them, telling them about any recent illnesses, allergies and medicines that you are currently using.

The team of doctors and nurses arrive at each new bivouac by aircraft and set up an extensive surgery from which they can treat most medical problems. At every bivouac location they will have set up a prior arrangement with a nearby civilian or military hospital. More medical personnel are out on the route in specially equipped cars and motorcycles and in the air a helicopter is used for fast response to any emergency situation.

While most competitors hope they do not need to use these facilities it is reassuring to know that the medical service is as good or better than you would get at a local event back in your own country.

The medics wait for customers

It's not difficult to forecast the consequences of failing to look after the race vehicle properly. The least of these may be that you simply come to a stop on the course and for some reason this always seems to happen at the worst place. Very few vehicles break down as they enter the evening bivouac. The worst situation is caused by a mechanical failure that results in an accident, where drivers get hurt.

To avoid problems with your vehicle you need to establish a procedure with your service crew. If you sign up with a service and assistance organisation you will find they do this automatically.

Firstly, as soon as you arrive at the assistance point you should report on any problems that you have experienced during the day's journey. Secondly, the service crew should attend to a list of routine items such as oil levels or an oil change, oil filters, air filters,

control cables, brake pads, chain condition, tyre changes; this list is very long. While working the mechanics will study every part of the vehicle looking for damage or component failure. On a car damage could be underneath and caused by rocks or on a bike it could be caused by a fall. Added to these outside influences are the problems of component fatigue caused by vibration on rough ground.

The important issue is that by establishing a procedure the mechanics can be sure that everything is done to ensure that the vehicle won't let you down and you, the competitor, have confidence in your mechanics.

Once out on the route and the special stages all repairs are your own responsibility except at any designated assistance points. Even if an assistance crew sees you stopped on the course they cannot help you, but another competitor can. Most cars have room to carry a selection of essential tools and a supply of useful spare parts. A motorcycle rider has limited storage space and the regulations forbid the carrying of tools or spare parts in haversacks, pockets or waist bags. The solution is to secure a tool bag, strong enough to stand the rigors of riding, to the rear mudguard. Breaking down and finding your bag empty means you are at the mercy of a friendly competitor.

Some motorcyclists strap spare inner tubes and heavy tools, such as an adjustable wrench, to the frame with plastic ties.

Should you break down it is important not to panic as this can only result in further lost time. Attend to the problem and try to do it correctly the first time, as driving on with a partly cured problem can only cause further damage.

Somewhere in the desert is a selection of essential tools

The tyre pressure was a little bit too low

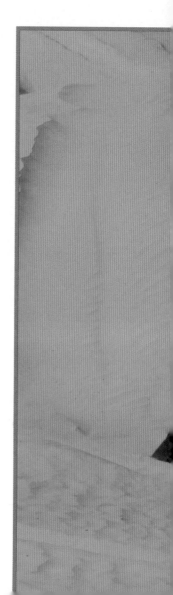

Once the 'bib mousse' breaks, an inner tube must be fitted into the tyre

Lawrence Noble gets a helping hand in the middle of nowhere

## Tyres

Competitors should arrange for their own supply of tyres, purchasing them in advance and organising carriage to the bivouacs. You cannot be certain of being able to purchase them during the event other than from the service crew of a retired competitor. The cost of carrying a large car tyre usually exceeds the cost of purchase, therefore if you do purchase one at a bivouac expect to pay more than double the usual price. Motorcycle competitors are allowed to have two wheels carried in a specially equipped aircraft but they will need at least ten more tyres and mousses and these must be transported by truck. Most car and truck competitors can carry at least two spare wheels that are already fitted with tyres while further tyres will also travel on an assistance truck.

Euromaster provide an essential service at every bivouac where anyone can take wheels and new tyres for fitting.

This aircraft carries four hundred motorcycle wheels & hundreds of steel boxes

Handy workbench!

# Euromaster

One of the main sponsors of the Dakar is the tyre and service organisation known as Euromaster or ATS in the UK. Each evening at the bivouac they provide a tyre fitting service for every competitor. Their two big trucks, numbered E1 and E2, travel along the assistance route and arrive at the bivouac in time to set up an impressive workshop. Brightly lit and usually close to the cafeteria it is one of the busiest places in the bivouac. Competitors and mechanics form a never-ending stream as they bring wheels of every size and description along with new tyres to the trained fitters. Making full use of the specialised equipment carried in the trucks they quickly remove the worn out tyre and fit the new one.

As a French company most of the mechanics naturally speak French but during the 2003 event a distinctive Liverpool accent could be heard above the babble. It belonged to Simon Heath who was experiencing his first Dakar rally. He managed to find a few minutes to explain how he came to be there in the middle of the Libyan Desert on a cold night. As an ATS branch manager he received a memo from his head office asking for volunteers who would like to spend three weeks working at the Dakar. Being a motorsport enthusiast he knew about the event and sent his application in as quickly as possible. The French-speaking requirement involved many weeks at night school.

In June he was advised that his application had been successful and that he should report to Clermont Ferrand to meet with the other members of the team and take part in a week long training session.

Naturally his colleagues at work thought that he was going for a free holiday. By the end of the event he realised how hard he had worked. He calculated that he had fitted more tyres of every size and type, many more than he would fit during a year at his Aintree depot. Despite the endless stream of wheels he was obviously enjoying himself, totally immersed in a world of enthusiasts drawn from more than thirty countries.

Each day the trucks with two drivers aboard would move to the next bivouac while an organisation aircraft was flying the fitters ahead. As this group arrived they would unroll their sleeping bags and get as much sleep as they could. When the trucks drove in they set up the working area ready for the arrival of the first support teams and their competitors. The whole team was then ready to work throughout the night if necessary.

## Fuel

The regulations for each event will state the minimum range for all vehicles and a percentage extra – usually ten percent is added. For example, in 2003 motorcycles and quads needed a minimum range of three hundred and fifty kilometres and other vehicles a range of eight hundred kilometres (five hundred miles). Any calculations of fuel consumption should be based on the worst type of terrain where low gears

will be used. Car and truck competitors and assistance crews are responsible for organising their own fuel throughout the event. All competitors should always leave each morning with a full tank of fuel, the carrying of spare fuel cans is prohibited. The road books show places where fuel is available and on the European mainland there are plenty of petrol stations along the route. It is also possible to fill up with fuel in villages along the route, but there is no guarantee that adequate supplies will be available and Total help by providing a map showing where their own stations are located. The organisers arrange for 200 litre drums of fuel to be available at bivouacs in areas where the supply is limited and competitors have to book and pay for their fuel in advance. Almost certainly the balancing act of buying as you go and collecting your supply at the bivouac will result in a nearly full, and paid for, drum of

Desert fuel stop for motorcycles

fuel being left behind. The fuel order for the Mitsubishi team at one of the Libyan bivouacs was for forty-six drums. Upon arrival at a bivouac one of the first tasks is to find the fuelling service and arrange for drums of fuel to be delivered to your car or truck.
An assistance team will already have made these arrangements on your behalf.

Motorcyclists and quad riders are in a more fortunate position as their fuel in Africa is charged for with their entry fee. During the day the road book will show the refuelling points which may be positioned along the liaison route or on the special stage. Riders are checked into a neutral zone where they can refuel and renew their water supply before being called to continue. On arrival at a bivouac they drive to the refuelling point where the fuel tanks are refilled.

## Total-Fina-Elf

Following a ten-year involvement as the major sponsor of the event, Total-Fina-Elf have stepped aside and become joint sponsors with Euromaster and Telefonica. In addition many individual competitors enjoy some direct help from a company that has commercial activities in most countries that the Dakar has visited. This has enabled them to produce a map that shows the location of their petrol stations that can be accessed from the route. This is particularly invaluable to assistance vehicles who usually don't rely on the official refuelling points.

In line with ASO's, the event organisers, policy of encouraging amateurs, Total run their own competition within the main competition. The Elf Motorcycle Trophy and the Total Car Trophy provide cash awards that are designed to reduce the financial outlay of amateurs and newcomers.

The Total-Fina-Elf website provides a constant service providing daily reports on the progress of the competitors, including those in the Elf and Total Trophies.

Filling rear fuel tanks on KTM

No.1. – Fabrizio Meoni takes on fuel

Assistance point

## World press

Television reporter Toby Moody reports back

The 'Dakar' is the world's greatest motorsport event and is reported by electronic and print media in over one hundred & eighty countries. The organisers recognise the importance of this coverage by providing a press office at the start, at every bivouac and at the finish. Each day an aircraft ferries most of the journalists on to the next overnight stop while others travel on the course itself or along the assistance route. Stories and television reports are filed everyday to agencies, broadcasting companies and newspapers.

Journalists get the news as it happens directly from the helicopters flying over the course and from the electronic updates that are relayed to the press office. The journalists watch

their laptop computer screens as the daily finishing order changes.

Other TV and radio crews are waiting to interview the competitors at the finish of the 'special' stages or at the assistance areas. Using the satellite dishes and transmitters these reports are then sent to editors all over the world for inclusion in daily programmes. Enthusiasts in France are able to watch three television programmes every day while in Britain Eurosport transmit a daily update and more than thirty hours of programmes.

Its all sent home by satellite dish

## Communications

The majority of people at the event are not in the least concerned about what is happening in the rest of the world or about reporting back to those at home. For those that are, the organisers provide limited communication services. Satellite pay phones are sited close to the press office, although expensive they provide the means for a quick conversation. At the same place you may use one of the laptop computers to access the internet, send e-mails to family, sponsors or your local press.

## Photographs

It is worth carrying a compact camera to record that stunning view that you may never see again or capture the atmosphere at the bivouac. Even top riders like Giovanni Sala who don't usually waste time on the course will stop to take some photos. There is an official photographic service that is a source of action shots. Maindru Photo offer an internet service where you can buy on line or alternatively you can request 'contact sheets' which show a small version of each picture. You may want to order a selection of pictures including other competitors, locations or dramatic action.

## Press

Many amateur competitors, and particularly newcomers, feel that most journalists are present at the competition solely to report on the top competitors. This isn't the case; anybody from the media is interested in unusual incidents,

interesting competitors or those with a story to tell. You should make sure that you seek them out at the start and at the bivouacs as it could result in unexpected coverage that would please a sponsor. This is also true of the television media and you can try to be in their shots when they interview somebody else. Make sure that all your sponsors' logos can be clearly seen even if the interviewer doesn't talk to you. Most of the teams and service organisations have press officers who will be reporting back to the national and local press and websites with stories about team members. They want to hear about your experiences and it is worth taking time to talk to them even if you are very busy.

## Clippings

While you are away at the event arrange for somebody to record the Eurosport coverage on television and to buy all papers and magazines with articles about the event. Even if you are not mentioned it will be your only chance to make a clippings file. It will be your memories, an incentive to go again or better still a tool to obtain future sponsorship.

A relaxed Giovanni Sala gives an interview

Joan 'Nani' Roma calls home

Another interview for Fabrizio Meoni

# Decision

The time might arrive when you have to make a difficult decision... should you struggle on or retire? The circumstances when you could find yourself in this situation vary enormously although if you are seriously hurt or your vehicle is damaged beyond repair then you have little choice but to retire.

Every competitor must consider the situation carefully, where you would go, how you will get your car or truck back home and whether struggling on to the next bivouac will actually improve your situation. To cope well in these conditions you should always carry a reasonable amount of money in US dollars or Euros. You may need cash to pay people to help get you and your vehicle to the nearest large town or port.

If you are competing on a motorcycle there are two sweeper trucks that travel along the course behind the competitors. In the case of a breakdown it is imperative that you remain with the machine as the truck will only find you if you are on the course and it could take until the following day before they reach all the retired riders. Once collected you and your bike are deposited at the next bivouac and the machine is placed in a compound.
Riders will be taken to the nearest place where transport can be arranged to Europe and machines are later shipped to Paris to await collection.

Bike recovery – No. 4. Joan 'Nani' Roma

Car and truck competitors will find themselves in a different situation, as the sweeper trucks will take you and your co-driver on to the bivouac but not your vehicle. At this point you are faced with a choice, should you leave the vehicle, take a GPS reading so you can find the location when you return. Alternatively, you can stay with the vehicle and try to make arrangements to get it repaired and taken to the nearest port. If you decide to stay you will be asked to sign a paper which absolves the organisation from further responsibility. There is a compromise situation whereby one driver stays and the other goes on to the bivouac, or the nearest town, where transport for the recovery of the vehicle can be arranged.

Finding transport, or arranging for a tow, is not difficult as in every small town or village there is somebody who will offer to help. Once your vehicle is at the port and arrangements have been made for shipment to Europe you have to find your own way home. All this is part of the adventure and can often prove to be one of the most interesting aspects of the whole experience.

Jose Luis Steuri's bike arrives on a police pick-up

# Alfie Cox

Alfie Cox from Cato Ridge, Nr Durban, South Africa had won everything in his home country before deciding to take on the rest of the world. He has won practically every South African enduro and rally event and championship, a total of twenty-five national championships. At the Dakar he has always ridden a KTM and came to prominence in 1998 with a third place and in 2002 he finished a close second to Fabrizio Meoni. He celebrates his birthday every year during the event and it would seem that it is only a matter of time before he achieves his ambition to win the event.

The expression on the face of Bradley Cox says it all

Note: happy birthday sticker on side of bike

# Jutta Kleinschmidt

Jutta Kleinschmidt, from Cologne, Germany's most successful lady competitor in desert rally racing. Not only is she the only woman to win the Dakar, she remains the only one able to compete at the highest level. Her Dakar experience began on motorcycles and success came early with a Ladies Cup win in the 1992 event, Paris-Le Cap Rallye. The following year she switched to the car category competing in Schlesser buggies.

High places in the World Cross-Country Cup and all the major rallies followed as she started to make an impact on the Dakar results. A change to Mitsubishi produced the result that she sought with a win in the 2001 event. For 2003 Jutta headed the new Volkswagen team with an all new buggy. At the finish Jutta was in eighth place and was the highest placed lady driver; a good result for the team.

The all new Volkswagen – with damaged front wheel on the first special stage

## Success

Every competitor who reaches the finish, no matter where they are placed in the results, will regard this as a triumph. Riding on to the podium and shaking hands with Hubert Auriol is something that they dreamt about when they shook hands with him on the start podium three weeks ago. It is usual for the service team to join their competitors on the podium and share in their celebrations.

Car driver Hiroshi Masouka and co-driver Andreas Schultz were victorious and all the Mitsubishi team members began to celebrate

The winning truck driver was Vladimir Tchaguire with his two co-drivers Semion Yakoubor
and Sergvei Savostine and all the Master Kamaz team crews were jubilant

Jose Manuel Pellicer from Spain was the Best
Newcomer Motorcyclist

Polish riders Jacek Czachor and Marek
Dabrowski celebrate their success

The Yamaha quad driver Josef Machacez is
happy to be on the finish podium

Best Car Newcomer prize was won by Christophe Tinseau and Baptiste Vallet driving a Ford Protruck

The RallyRaid UK 4x4 truck was driven all the way to the finish podium by Frenchman Michel Saumer and co-driver Roma O'Epremesnil

Spaniards Fernando Gill and Raphael Santinen enjoy success with their Telefonica sponsored Mercedes ML340

# Getting home

The next task is to get your vehicle home and the organisers can make all the arrangements. If you have used a complete package, such as that provided by RallyRaid UK, they will be responsible for making all the arrangements. All the motorcycles and quads are placed in containers for transport to the nearest port where they will be taken to Paris. Cars and trucks must be driven to a specified port to await shipment by boat to a European mainland port where they will be stored. All competitors will be advised when the vehicles are back in Europe and you must make the necessary arrangements for collection.

*Sorting out personal luggage*

All that remains is for you to enjoy the celebrations and then catch the flight back to Paris and the ongoing flight to your home country. Both these can be booked and paid for through the VSO travel agency at the finish.

Gordon McPhereson and Derrick Edmondson pack their box for shipment back to Europe

Competitors return the GPS equipment at the finish

## Sponsors

Competing in the Dakar and experiencing the adventure of crossing the wide expanses of the desert has a marked effect on most people. As a result it is very easy in the euphoria of relating your experiences to family and friends to forget about the people who provided help. Contacting them a month later is not the answer.

As soon as possible you should write a short letter or a thank you note to all your sponsors and to the team members who helped you at the event. Contact the website of the official photographers and buy some good action photographs of yourself, which can be framed and presented to your sponsors. Provided your sponsors aren't too far away deliver these personally and ask if they will help again next year. The friendships begun during the event with foreign competitors and team-mates can progress via e-mail. Begin to write a journal and make a scrapbook with press cuttings and photographs to record your adventure, which you can later use to attract even more sponsors for next year.

A photo for the sponsors

# Appendices

- Results

- Acknowledgements

- Useful Addresses

# Results

## Motorcycles

### 1979
1. Neveu C. (Fra) Yamaha
2. Comte G. (Fra) Yamaha
3. Vassard P. (Fra) Honda

### 1980
1. Neveu C. (Fra) Yamaha
2. Merel M. (Fra) Yamaha
3. Pineau J-N. (Fra) Yamaha

### 1981
1. Auriol H. (Fra) BMW
2. Bacou S. (Fra) Yamaha
3. Merel M. (Fra) Yamaha

### 1982
1. Neveu C. (Fra) Honda
2. Vassard P. (Fra) Honda
3. Verhaegue G. (Fra) Barigo

### 1983
1. Auriol H. (Fra) BMW
2. Drobecq P. (Fra) Honda
3. Joineau M. (Fra) Suzuki

### 1984
1. Rahier G. (Bel) BMW
2. Auriol H. (Fra) BMW
3. Vassard P. (Fra) Honda

### 1985
1. Rahier G. (Bel) BMW
2. Olivier J-C. (fra) Yamaha
3. Picco F. (Ita) Yamaha

### 1986
1. Neveu C. (Fra) Honda
2. Lalay G. (Fra) Honda
3. Balestrieri A. (Ita) Honda

### 1987
1. Neveu C. (Fra) Honda
2. Orioli E. (Ita) Honda
3. Rahier (Bel) BMW

### 1988
1. Orioli E. (Ita) Honda
2. Picco F. (Ita) Yamaha
3. Lalay (Fra) Honda

### 1989
1. Lalay G. (Fra) Honda
2. Picco F. (Ita) Yamaha
3. Morales F. (Fra) Honda

### 1990
1. Orioli E. (Ita) Cagiva
2. Mas S. (Esp) Yamaha
3. De Petri (Ita) Cagiva

### 1991
1. Peterhansel S. (Fra) Yamaha
2. Lalay G. (Fra) Yamaha
3. Magnaldi T. (Fra) Yamaha

### 1992
1. Peterhansel S. (Fra) Yamaha
2. Laporte D. (US) Cagiva
3. Arcarons J. (Esp) Cagiva

### 1993
1. Peterhansel S. (Fra) Yamaha
2. Charbonnier S. (Fra) Yamaha
3. Arcarons J. (Esp) Yamaha

### 1994
1. Orioli E. (Ita) Cagiva
2. Arcarons J. (Esp) Cagiva
3. Meoni F. (Ita) Honda

### 1995
1. Peterhansel S. (Fra) Yamaha
2. Arcarons J. (Esp) Cagiva
3. Orioli E. (Ita) Cagiva

### 1996
1. Orioli E. (Ita) Yamaha
2. Arcarons J. (Esp) KTM
3. Sotelo (Esp) KTM

### 1997
1. Peterhansel S. (Fra) Yamaha
2. Gallardo O. (Esp) Cagiva
3. Castera P. (Fra) Yamaha

### 1998
1. Peterhansel S. (Fra) Yamaha
2. Meoni F. (I) KTM
3. Cox A. (SA) KTM

**1999**
1. Sainct R. (Fra) BMW
2. Magnaldi (Fra) KTM
3. Cox A. (SA) KTM

**2000**
1. Sainct R. (Fra) BMW
2. Gallardo O. (Esp) BMW
3. Lewis J. (USA) BMW

**2001**
1. Meoni F. (I) KTM
2. Acarons J. (Esp) KTM
3. De Gavardo (Ch) KTM

**2002**
1. Meoni F. (I ) KTM
2. Cox A. (SA) KTM
3. Sainct R. (Fra) KTM

**2003**
1. Sainct R. (Fra) KTM
2. Despres C. (Fra) KTM
3. Meoni F. (I) KTM

# Cars

**1979**
1. Genestier/Terblaut/Lemordant (Fra) Range Rover
2. Marreau/Marreau (Fra) Renault
3. Giraudo/Cavalleri (Ita) Fiat

**1980**
1. Kotulinsky/Luffelman (Ger) Volkswagen
2. Zaniroli/Colesse (Fra) Volkswagen
3. Marreau/Marreau (Fra) Renault

**1981**
1. Metge/Giroux (Fra) Range Rover
2. Cotel/Corbetta (Fra) Buggy
3. Briavoine/Boulanger (Fra) Lada

**1982**
1. Marreau/Marreau (Fra) Renault
2. Briavoine/Deliatre (Fra) Lada
3. Jausaud/Briere (Fra) Mercedes

**1983**
1. Ickx/Brasseur (Bel) Mercedes
2. Trossat/Briovoine (Fra) Lada
3. Lartigue/Destailats (Fra) Range Rover

**1984**
1. Metge/Lemoyne (Fra) Porche
2. Zaniroli/Da Silva (Fra) Range Rover
3. Cowan/Syer (GB) Mitsubishi

**1985**
1. Zaniroli/Da Silva (Fra) Mitsubishi
2. Cowan/Syer (GB) Mitsubishi
3. Fougerouse/Jaquemar (Fra) Toyota

**1986**
1. Metge/Lemoyne (Fra) Porche
2. Ickx/Brasseur (Bel) Porche
3. Rigal/Maingret (Fra) Mitsubishi

**1987**
1. Vatanen/Giroux (Fin) Peugeot
2. Zaniroli/Lopes (Fra) Range Rover
3. Shinozuka/Fenouil (Jap) Mitsubishi

**1988**
1. Kankkunen/Pironen (Fin) Peugeot
2. Shinozuka/Magne (Jap) Mitsubishi
3. Tambay/Lemoyne (Fra) Range Rover

**1989**
1. Vatanen/Berger (Fin) Peugeot
2. Ickx/Tarin (Bel) Peugeot
3. Tambay/Lemoyne (Fra) Mitsubishi

**1990**
1. Vatanen/Berglund (Fin) Peugeot
2. Waldegard/Fenouil (Swe) Peugeot
3. Ambrosino/Gaurngartner (Fra) Peugeot

# Results

1991
1. Vatanen/Berglund (Fin) Citroën
2. Lartigue/Destaillats (Fra) Mitsubishi
3. Fontenay/Musmarra (Fra) Mitsubishi

1992
1. Auriol/Monnet (Fra) Mitsubishi
2. Weber/Hiemer (Ger) Mitsubishi
3. Shinozuka/Magne (Jap) Mitsubishi

1993
1. Saby/Serieys (Fra) Mitsubishi
2. Lartigue/Perin (Fra) Citroën
3. Auriol/Picard (Fra) Citroën

1994
1. Lartigue/Perin (Fra) Citroën
2. Auriol/Picard (Fra) Citroën
3. Wambergue/Cottret (Fra) Bourgo

1995
1. Lartigue/Perin (Fra) Citroën
2. Saby/Serieys (Fra) Mitsubishi
3. Shinozuka/Magne (Jap) Mitsubishi

1996
1. Lartigue/Perin (Fra) Citroën
2. Wambergue/Gallagher (Fra) Citroën
3. Fontenay/Musmarra (Fra) Mitsubishi

1997
1. Shinozuka/Magne (Jap) Mitsubishi
2. Fontenay/Musmarra (Fra) Mitsubishi
3. Saby/Serieys (Fra) Mitsubishi

1998
1. Fontenay/Picard (Fra) Mitsubishi
2. Shinozuka/Magne (Jap) Mitsubishi
3. Saby/Serieys (Esp) Mitsubishi

1999
1. Schlesser/Monnet (Fra) Schlesser Renault
2. Prieto/Serieys (Esp) Mitsubishi
3. Kleinschmidt/Thorner (Ger) Mitsubishi

2000
1. Schlesser/Magne (Fra) Schlesser Renault
2. Peterhansel/Cottret (Fra) SBM
3. Fontenay/Picard (Fra) Mitsubishi

2001
1. Kleinschmidt/Schulz (Ger) Mitsubishi
2. Masuoka/Maimon (Jap) Mitsubishi
3. Schlesser/Magne (Ger) Schlesser Renault

2002
1. Masuoka/Maimon (Jap) Mitsubishi
2. Kleinschmidt/Schulz (Ger) Mitsubishi
3. Shinozuka/Delli-Zotti (Jap) Mitsubishi

2003
1. Masuoka/Schulz (Jap) Mitsubishi
2. Fontenay/Picard (Fra) Mitsubishi
3. Peterhansel/Cottret (Fra) Mitsubishi

# Acknowledgements

Photographs:

Dorothy Jones
Maindru Photo
Andrew Neri
BMW (GB)
DPPI


Information:

Amaury Sport Organisation
RallyRaid UK
Total-Fina-Elf
Euromaster
Telefonica

# Useful Addresses

Amaury Sport Organisation (ASO). (Organisers of the Dakar Rally).
2 rue Rouget de Lisle – F-92130 – ISSY-LES-MOULINEAUX
Tel: +33 (0) 1 41 33 14 60/62      Fax: +33 (0) 1 41 33 14 69
www.Dakar.com

RallyRaid UK. (The British Service and Support Organisation).
Houndgate Lodge, Lower Cumberworth,
Nr. Huddersfield. West Yorkshire. HD8 8PL
Tel: +44 (0) 1484 86 12 38
www.rallyraid.co.uk

Maindru Photo. (The official Dakar photographers).
6, rue Jules Dauban. B.P. 1827. 49018 Angers Cedex 01. France
Tel: +33 (0) 2 41 88 05 85      Fax: +33 (0) 2 41 87 71 87
www.maindruphoto.com

Euromaster. (Official tyre fitters at the Dakar Rally).
www.euromaster.com

KTM Sportsmotorcycles. (Spare parts support at the Dakar Rally).
www.ktm.com

## The Authors

Dot & Jim have been married for over forty years after first meeting at a motorcycle training course in Liverpool. Along with their two sons and three grandchildren they have continued to be involved in off-road motorsport.

They are now based in mid Wales. With more time to travel they are still eager for new experiences. They know that life is not a rehearsal, it is the main event.